Contents

Animals in the wild

There are lots of different wild animals.

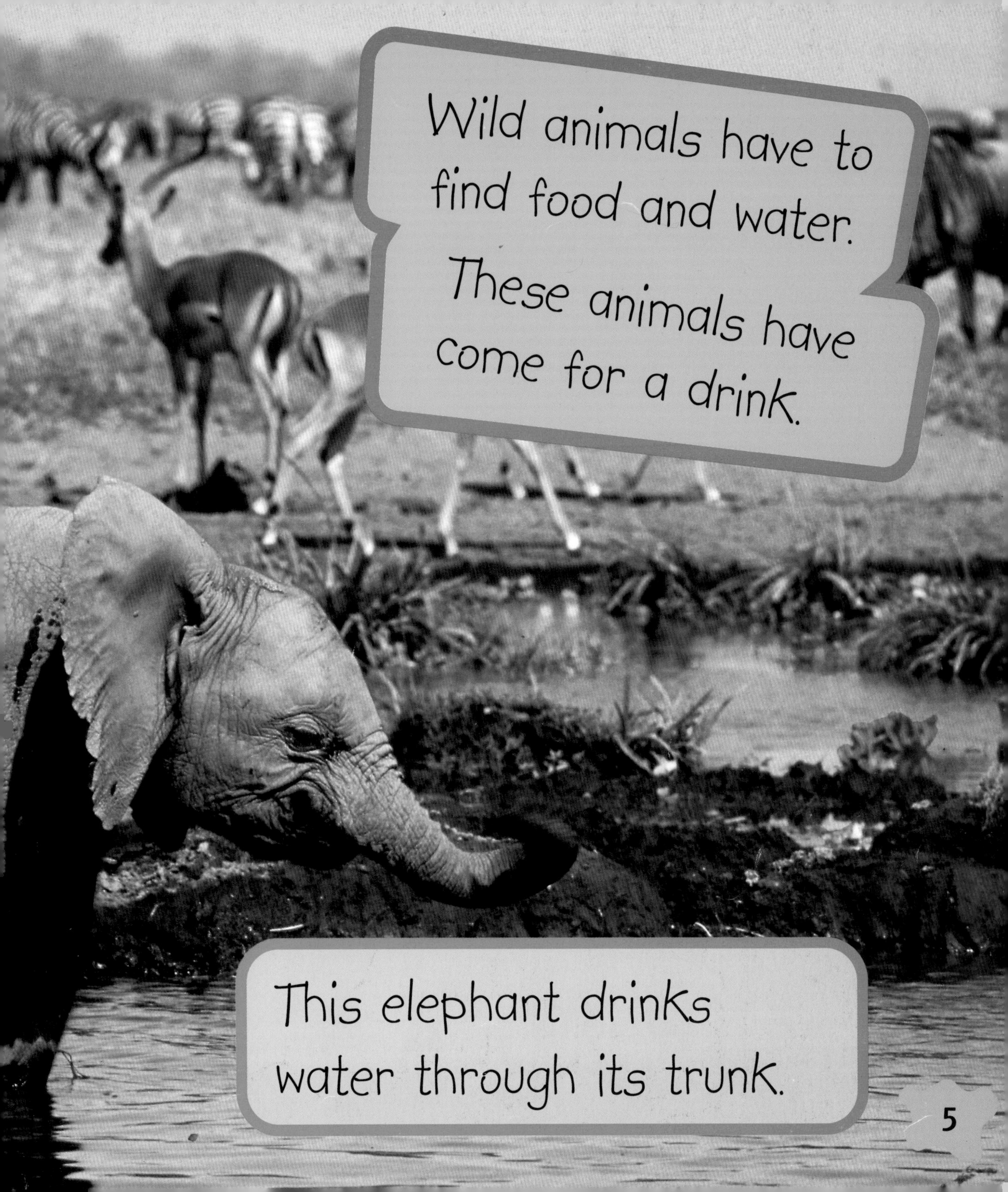

Wild animals have to find food and water. These animals have come for a drink.

This elephant drinks water through its trunk.

Different wild animals

Wild animals come in all shapes and sizes.

This big bear lives in the mountains.

Squirrels live in many different places.

Do you know what squirrels like to eat?

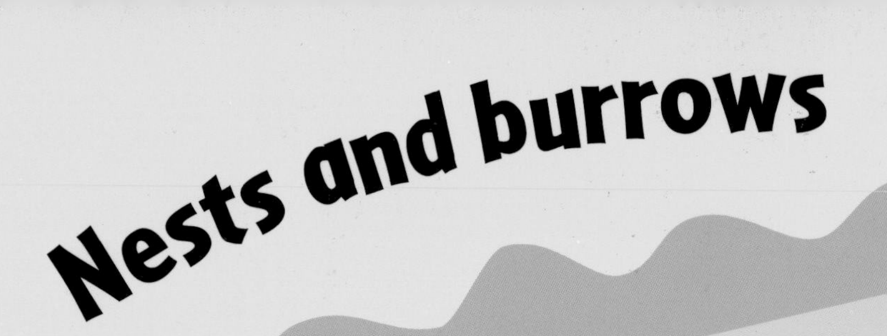

Nests and burrows

Some wild animals make their homes under the ground.

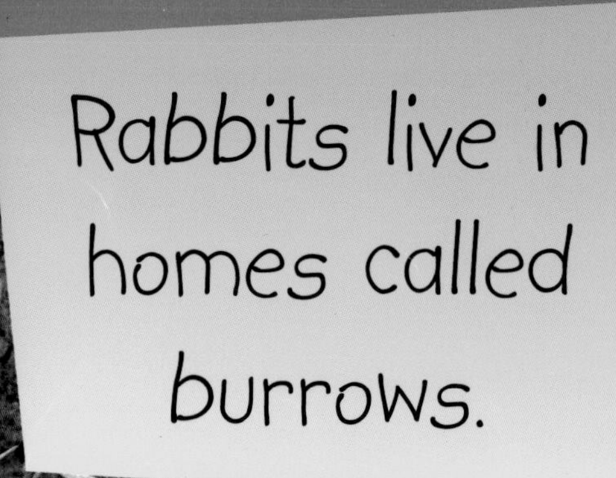

Rabbits live in homes called burrows.

This animal is called
a raccoon. It makes its
nest high up in a tree.

Food and water

Wild animals need food to stay healthy.

Giraffes have long necks to reach leaves high in the trees.

All animals need water to drink. This bird drinks from a pool.

Animals in the air

Some animals have wings and can fly.

Bats fly around at night.

Many birds fly in big groups called flocks.

What do you think these gulls are looking for?

Animals in the water

Some wild animals live underwater.

These fish live in the ocean. They swim around the coral to look for food.

Moving around

Kangaroos have strong back legs for hopping along.

BOING!

Orangutans have long arms for swinging through trees.
Dolphins use their tails to push them through the water.

Making noises

Wild animals make all kinds of noises.

Wolves howl.

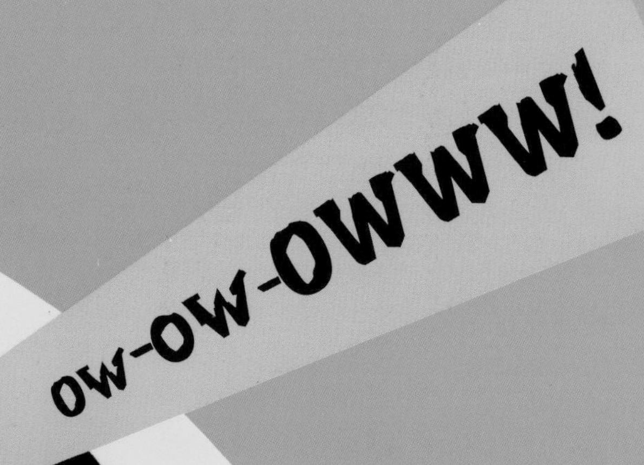

Tigers growl.

GRRRRR!

Can you squawk like a parrot?

SQUAWK!

Baby wild animals

Animals take care of their babies.

These polar bear cubs stay close to their mother.

Birds find food for their young.

This bird caught a caterpillar for her babies to eat.

Caring and cleaning

Wild animals take good care of each other.

Lions use their tongues to lick their fur clean.

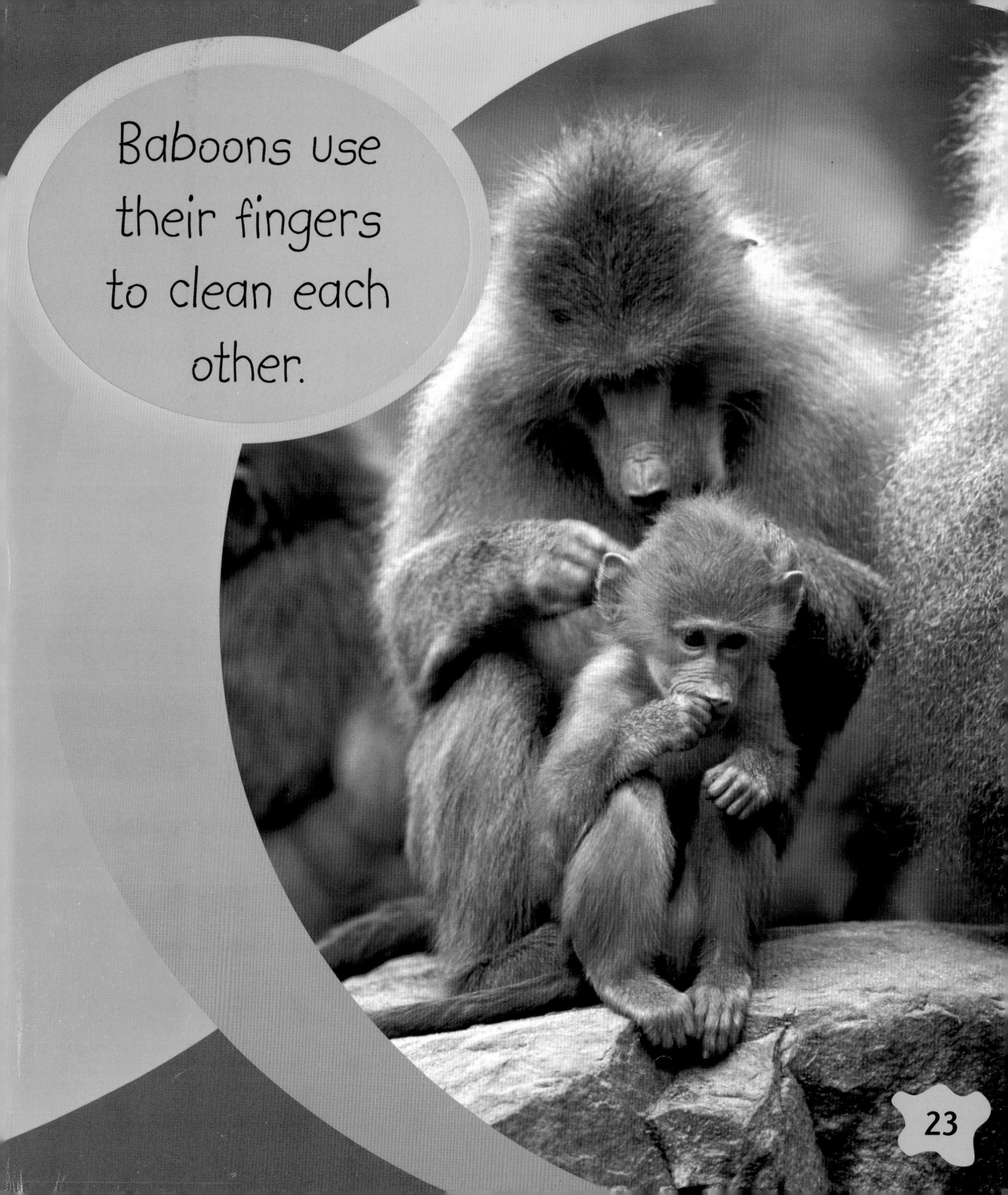

Baboons use their fingers to clean each other.

Index

Notes for adults

This series supports a young child's knowledge and understanding of their world. The following Early Learning Goals are relevant to the series:

- Find out about, and identify, some features of living things, objects, and events that they observe.
- Develop communication, language and literacy by imitating different animal sounds, and to notice and describe similarities and differences.

These books will help children extend their vocabulary, as they will hear some new words. Since words are used in context in the book this should enable young children to gradually incorporate them into their own vocabulary.

This series investigates a variety of animals by looking at distinguishing features and characteristics and by exploring their different environments.

Follow-up activities:

Encourage children to think about any wild animals they have seen in parks and gardens, and to draw a picture of their favourite animal and where it lives.